# Human Nature Unveiled:

## Navigating the Tapestry of Four Behavioral Archetypes

Richard L. Collins

<u>Conclusion</u>
- <u>Summing Up Behavioral Diversity</u>
- <u>Encouraging Inclusivity</u>

# <u>Introduction</u>

## *<u>An Overview of Human Behavior:</u>*

## *<u>Piecing Together the Sequence of</u>*
## *<u>Actions and Reactions</u>*

Deciphering human behavior is like trying to unravel a complicated tapestry made of individual experiences, environment, and heredity. Human behavior is made up of a wide range of acts, responses, ideas, and feelings that influence how we interact with the outside world and with one another.

Human behavior is fundamentally the result of the dynamic interaction between nature and nurture. Environmental variables, such as culture, upbringing, and life experiences, shape and refine innate inclinations, whereas biological elements, such as genetics and neurochemistry, provide the basis for certain predispositions. The result is a wide range of

actions that set one person apart from the other.

Investigating the terrain of human behavior necessitates exploring several facets. Every aspect of human behavior, from the mental processes guiding choices to the subtle emotional dynamics forming relationships, adds to the complex tapestry of behavior. Furthermore, the social environment is crucial in shaping behavior at the individual and group levels.

This synopsis lays the groundwork for a more thorough investigation of the four main categories of human conduct. Driver, Evaluative, Compliant, and Communicative. We will traverse the nuances and intricacies that characterize people's thought processes, modes of communication, and interactions with the outside world as we set off on our adventure. Understanding the complexities of human behavior helps us negotiate the different fabric of people with empathy and respect. It also fosters understanding.

# The Importance of Recognizing Behavioral Diversity

In the fabric of human relationships, the importance of understanding behavioral variation is fundamental to establishing deep connections, productive dialogue, and peaceful cooperation. Behavioral variety has to be understood for the following main reasons:

**1. Improved Communication**: others may communicate ideas more successfully when they are aware of the many communication styles that others use.
Communication may be made clearer and less confusing by adapting to the preferences of various behavioral types.

**2. Optimized Team Dynamics:** Innovative and well-rounded problem-solving are fostered in teams made up of persons with a variety of behavioral talents.

Recognizing the inclinations of team members helps create a positive atmosphere where everyone's abilities may be used to achieve success as a group.

**3. _Effective Leadership:_** Leaders who are aware of behavioral variety can modify their approaches so that they inspire and connect with their team.

- Leaders may build motivated and cohesive teams by identifying and valuing the unique abilities within their team.

**4. _Conflict Resolution:_** By focusing on the root causes of problems rather than just the obvious ones, awareness of different behaviors helps resolve disagreements.

- Promoting empathy and open communication helps to resolve conflicts productively.

**5. _Enhanced Inclusivity and Empathy:_** Empathy is fostered by realizing that individuals approach relationships and tasks in various ways.

- Accepting behavioral variety promotes an inclusive workplace where people are respected for their contributions.

**6. _Personal Growth:_** - Understanding one's behavioral inclinations might help one grow personally.

Continuous learning and adaptation are made possible by the ability to identify and adjust to a variety of behaviors.

Essentially, the importance of comprehending behavioral variety is found in creating connections that foster respect and understanding across a wide range of human actions. Interpersonal dynamics are turned from possible points of contention into chances for cooperation, development, and mutual success. By recognizing and appreciating the variety of conduct, we build a more robust and peaceful human fabric.

# Chapter 1.

# Foundations of Human Behavior

## *Perspectives on the Past: historic*

The study of human behavior may be traced back through the millennia, resonating with the inquisitiveness of ancient philosophers and intellectuals who endeavored to solve the mystery of human nature. Plato and Aristotle were two of the most influential people in ancient Greece, and they were both involved in arguments on ethics, emotions and the development of character. It was through these meditations that the foundation was built for understanding human conduct about moral and societal constraints.

Perspectives on human conduct changed in tandem with the development of civilizations. During the Renaissance period, there was a renaissance of interest in humanism, which emphasized the investigation of human potential and the unique experiences of people. Philosophers such as John Locke and Jean-Jacques Rousseau made significant contributions to the discussion on the interplay between nature and nurture during the Enlightenment period, which further accelerated the scientific investigation of human behavior.

During the 19th century, the field of psychology emerged as a separate discipline from other disciplines. Through the development of his psychoanalytic theory, Sigmund Freud was the first person to propose the concept of the unconscious mind and the effect of early events on conduct. Concurrently, behaviorism, pioneered by people like John B. Watson and B.F. Skinner, turned the emphasis to observable actions, steering away from interior mental processes.

# *Theories and Models:*

The 20th century brought a profusion of ideas and models that claimed to encompass the intricacies of human behavior. One notable model is Maslow's Hierarchy of demands, which argues that human drives follow a hierarchical pattern, spanning from fundamental physiological demands to higher-level ideals like self-actualization.

Erik Erikson's Psychosocial Development Theory expanded this knowledge to embrace the lifetime, distinguishing phases of psychosocial development and the related crises that affect personality. These ideas stress the dynamic interaction between biological, psychological, and social elements in influencing behavior.

Cognitive theories, such as those offered by Jean Piaget, focused on mental processes, stressing the significance of cognitive development in determining behavior.

Piaget's stages of cognitive development explain how humans gain information and understanding as they advance through various developmental periods.

In the field of personality, the Five-Factor Model (Big Five) gained popularity. This model highlights five major dimensions—Openness, Conscientiousness, Extraversion, Agreeableness, and Neuroticism—that contribute to individual variations in behavior and personality.

Contemporary theories contain a more comprehensive view of human behavior, emphasizing the effect of cultural and social settings. Social Cognitive Theory, created by Albert Bandura, stresses observational learning and the relevance of social interactions in behavior acquisition.

As we traverse the vast fabric of human behavior, these historical viewpoints and varied ideas serve as guideposts, representing the growth of thinking and our unceasing effort to fathom the nuances of what makes us uniquely human. The underpinnings of human behavior weaved through time and theory, continue to define the dynamic fabric of psychological research.

# <u>Chapter 2:</u>

# <u>Driver Behavior</u>

## *<u>Navigating with Determination and Decisiveness</u>*

Driver conduct is defined as a deliberate and goal-oriented attitude to activities and problems. Individuals with a primary driving behavior display a strong desire to achieve objectives, typically taking control and making choices with a focus on efficiency and effectiveness.

## *<u>Key Characteristics</u>*

*<u>1. Assertiveness</u>*: Drivers are forceful and proactive in achieving their aims. They are not scared to take leadership and make judgments promptly.

*<u>2. Goal-oriented:</u>* A strong sense of purpose motivates persons with driving behavior.

They are driven by objectives and thrive on finishing things.

**_3. Decisiveness:_** Quick decision-making is a feature of driving conduct. These folks seek to cut through complications and find answers swiftly.

**_4. Outcomes-driven:_** Drivers are outcome-focused and seek for demonstrable outcomes. They are driven by a feeling of success and growth.

**_5. High Energy_:** Often energetic and dynamic, persons with driver behavior tackle things with passion and zeal.

## *Communication Style*

Direct and to the point, drivers prefer succinct communication that highlights crucial information and goals.

- They may stress efficiency above detailed details, striving for concise and practical information.

# <u>Strengths</u>

- <u>***Leadership***</u>: Drivers readily take on leadership responsibilities, directing and pushing others toward accomplishing shared objectives.

- <u>***Initiative***</u>: Proactively taking control, drivers are quick to spot possibilities and difficulties, moving projects ahead.

- <u>***Problem-addressing***</u>: Decisiveness and a results-oriented mentality make drivers effective at addressing difficulties efficiently.

# <u>*Potential Challenges*</u>:

- <u>***irritation:***</u> A predisposition to emphasize speed may lead to irritation with procedures or persons regarded as hindering progress.

- <u>***Overlooking nuances***</u>: In their emphasis on results, drivers may sometimes ignore delicate nuances that might affect outcomes.

- <u>***Assertiveness Perception:***</u> The aggressive personality of drivers may be viewed as unduly domineering in some circumstances.

Understanding driver behavior is vital for successful teamwork. Leveraging their skills while addressing possible hurdles enables them to channel the tenacity and energy these folks bring to diverse pursuits.

# **Chapter 3**

# **Analytical Behavior**

## *Unraveling the Precision of Thought*

## *Characteristics*

***1. Logical Precision:*** Analytical persons thrive in logical thinking, handling difficulties with a deliberate and systematic perspective.

***2. Detail-Oriented:*** Their attention to detail is unsurpassed, as they thoroughly review material to verify correctness and completeness.

***3. Critical Thinking:*** Analytical thinkers show a great ability for critical thinking, dissecting situations to uncover core causes and ideal solutions.

**_4. Fact-Based Decision-Making:_** Preferring data over intuition, analytical persons base their conclusions on facts and evidence.

**_5. Structured Approach:_** They thrive in structured situations, frequently building organized methods to simplify procedures and boost efficiency.

**_6. Reserved Demeanor:_** While attentive and involved, persons with analytical conduct may look reserved, as they devote energy to thorough analysis.

## _Communication Style_

**_1. Clarity and Precision:_** Analytical communicators appreciate clarity, communicating concepts with precision and avoiding ambiguity.

**_2. Emphasis on Data:_** They depend on data-driven communication, offering facts and numbers to back their claims.

**_3. Detailed Explanations:_** When presenting knowledge, analytical persons offer detailed explanations, leaving no possibility for misunderstanding.

**_4. Objective and Detached:_** Their communication style tends to be objective and detached, focused on the content of the message.

**_5. Prefer Written Communication:_** Written communication helps them to explain concepts thoroughly, assuring clarity in their remarks.

**_6. Selective Verbal Expression:_** While not too chatty, analytical folks contribute to debates with intelligent and well-thought-out remarks.

# *Strengths:*

*1. Problem-Solving Prowess:* Analytical thinkers thrive at dissecting difficult issues and developing efficient answers.

*2. Planning and Organization:* Their ability to plan and arrange information is a vital advantage in both personal and professional situations.

*3. Attention to Detail:* Meticulous attention to detail boosts the quality and accuracy of the job.

*4. Research and Analysis:* Proficient in research, they acquire and evaluate information extensively to guide decision-making.

*5. Objective Decision-Making*: Embracing objectivity, analytical persons make judgments based on intellectual appraisal rather than emotional impulses.

**6. _Ongoing Learning:_** The hunger for information and a desire for ongoing development motivate their dedication to learning and being informed.

# _Potential Challenges:_

**1. _Overanalysis:_** There is a danger of overanalyzing circumstances, resulting in hesitation or delays in taking action.

**2. _Difficulty Delegating:_** The propensity to preserve control may result in issues when it comes to delegating work.

**3. _Less Adaptability to Ambiguity:_** Uncomfortable with ambiguity, analytical persons may struggle in circumstances lacking clear facts or knowledge.

4. Interpersonal difficulty: A reserved approach may cause difficulty in creating rapport or relating emotionally with people.

5. Perfectionism: Striving for perfection may lead to high self-imposed standards, producing stress and possibly burnout.

6. Less Tolerance for unrealistic Ideas: They may express doubt or fight ideas that are unrealistic or lack a strong basis.

Understanding analytical conduct uncovers a worldview strongly steeped in accuracy, logic, and strategic thinking. These people contribute essential traits to problem-solving circumstances, where their careful approach may lead to well-informed judgments.

# Chapter 4

# Amiable Behavior

Amiable conduct is defined as a kind, helpful, and cooperative attitude in interpersonal relationships. Individuals with pleasant features tend to value connections and harmony. They are sympathetic listeners, displaying a genuine concern for others' well-being. The communication style associated with pleasant conduct is frequently warm, polite, and focused on developing relationships.

## *Key Characteristics of Amiable Behavior:*

*1. Supportive*: Amiable persons are noted for offering emotional support and encouragement to others around them. They establish an environment of trust and understanding.

**_2. Cooperative:_** Collaboration is a cornerstone of agreeable conduct. These folks flourish in team environments, appreciating group dynamics and collaborative successes.

**_3. Empathetic:_** Understanding and sharing the sentiments of others comes effortlessly to persons with pleasant dispositions. They are responsive to the emotional needs of others around them.

**_4. Patient:_** Amiable persons generally display patience, both in coping with obstacles and in comprehending diverse views. They avoid quick judgments and conclusions.

## <u>*Communication Style:*</u>

- Amiable communicators take a polite and considerate approach. They seek to preserve pleasant connections, frequently employing non-confrontational language.
- Listening is a strength, as they seek to understand others' viewpoints and foster open dialogue.
- Expressing praise and thankfulness is widespread in their conversation, leading to a healthy and supportive workplace.

Strengths of Amiable Behavior: - Effective team player: Amiable individuals contribute to a collaborative and cohesive team environment.
- Strong interpersonal skills: Their capacity to connect with others develops healthy connections.
- Conflict resolution: Amiable persons excel at resolving problems by fostering understanding and compromise.

# *<u>Potential Challenges</u>*

- Difficulty making harsh choices: The desire for peace may lead to caution in making decisions that might destroy relationships.
- Avoidance of conflicts: While conflict avoidance helps sustain peace, it may delay resolving critical concerns.

Understanding pleasant conduct gives useful insights into creating healthy relationships, productive cooperation, and a supportive social environment. It stresses the significance of empathy, teamwork, and maintaining a healthy balance in human relationships.

# Chapter 5

# Expressive Behavior

## *Characteristics & Traits:*

Expressive behavior is marked by individuals who are outgoing, enthusiastic, and spontaneous in their approach to life. These folks frequently radiate vitality and thrive in social environments. Key features and attributes connected with expressive conduct include:

1. ***Enthusiastic:*** Expressive persons demonstrate a high degree of energy and excitement, providing a vivid and energetic presence in social interactions.

2. ***Outgoing:*** They are socially outgoing, loving the company of others, and actively pursuing social events.

**_3. Spontaneous:_** Expressive persons tend to welcome unpredictability, typically adjusting swiftly to changing conditions and embracing the excitement of new experiences.

**_4. Emotional Expression_**: They express their thoughts and feelings openly, wearing their emotions on their sleeve.

## _Communication techniques:_

Expressive communicators are noted for their energetic and engaging communication techniques. Their interactions are generally defined by the following:

**_1. Storytelling_**: Expressive folks like sharing tales and anecdotes, utilizing colorful language to engage their audience.

**_2. Animated Gestures:_** Their communication is complemented by expressive body language and gestures, adding emphasis and dynamism to their messages.

**_3._ _Persuasive:_** They possess strong persuasion skills, using charm and charisma to influence and inspire others.

**_4._ _Emphasis_ _on_ _Emotion_**: Expressive communicators deliver messages with emotion, making their conversation interesting and relevant.

# _Strengths:_

Expressive behavior brings forth several strengths that contribute to various aspects of personal and professional life:

**_1. Creativity_**: Expressive persons generally exhibit a creative flare, bringing fresh ideas and solutions to the table.

**_2. Motivational Leadership:_** They thrive at encouraging and inspiring others, creating an enthusiastic and vibrant team environment.

### 3. *Strong Communication Skills:* Expressive persons are great communicators, making them competent at communicating ideas and developing relationships.

# *Challenges*

While expressive behavior has its strengths, it also presents certain challenges that individuals may need to navigate:

*1. Impulsivity:* The spontaneous character of expressive persons may often lead to impulsive decision-making.

*2. Attention to Detail:* In their enthusiasm, they may overlook finer details, requiring mindfulness in certain situations.

Understanding expressive behavior provides insights into harnessing the strengths of these individuals in collaborative endeavors, while also being mindful of potential challenges that may arise in specific contexts. This chapter intends to study the dynamics of expressive conduct, giving practical insights for managing interpersonal and professional encounters.

# Chapter 6

# Intersectionality and Behavior

In this chapter, we dig into the notion of intersectionality—a prism through which we perceive the intricate interaction of multiple components of human identity and how they intersect to create behavior. Intersectionality believes that people possess various identities and experiences that may impact their behavior concurrently.

## *Recognizing Overlapping qualities:*

### *1. Complex Interplay of Traits:*
Intersectionality in behavior admits that people typically display a mix of behavioral qualities from multiple categories. This

interaction provides a rich tapestry of qualities that contribute to the complexity of human behavior.

**2. _Influence of Environment_**: Overlapping features are formed not just by individual predispositions but also by the dynamic interaction with cultural, social, and environmental influences. These aspects contribute to the flexibility and adaptability of behavior.

**3. _Nuanced Communication Styles_**: Individuals with overlapping features may display nuanced communication styles, drawing on the strengths of numerous behavior types. This versatility boosts their capacity to interact with a varied spectrum of persons.

**4. _Synergy in Team Dynamics:_** Recognizing overlapping tendencies becomes critical in team dynamics, as people with varied but intersecting behaviors may complement one

another, leading to more robust problem-solving and creativity.

**5. *Adaptive Leadership***: Leaders with overlapping attributes may traverse varied difficulties more successfully. Their capacity to draw on multiple behavioral strengths helps them adjust their leadership approach to varied scenarios and team compositions.

**6. *Understanding multiple Identities:*** Embracing overlapping features develops a greater understanding of people's multiple identities. This acknowledgment is crucial in encouraging inclusion and valuing the unique contributions each individual contributes to a particular situation.

# *Individual Variation:*

**_1. Personal Context Matters_**: Individual variation understands that behavior is extremely contextual and may change depending on personal experiences, life stages, and shifting situations. What may be a dominating quality in one context may take a back seat in another.

**_2. Cultural Influences:_** Cultural origins greatly affect individual variance in behavior. Different cultural norms and beliefs impact how people show their qualities and manage social relationships.

**_3. Developmental Changes_**: Behavior undergoes natural evolution during the lifetime. Understanding individual variation includes knowing that qualities may appear differently at various phases of life.

**_4. Unique Personality mixes_**: People display unique mixes of qualities, generating a broad spectrum of behavior. This individual variance adds to the complexity of human interactions and relationships.

**_5. Adaptability and Resilience:_** Individuals with a capacity for individual variation display adaptability and resilience in the face of changing circumstances. This versatility helps their capacity to negotiate varied social settings.

**_6. Impact of External influences:_** External influences, such as stresses or life events, might impact individual behavior. Recognizing individual variation includes knowing how external stimuli may temporarily alter or change behavioral patterns.

This chapter addresses the complicated dynamics of intersectionality and individual variety in behavior, offering insight into the complexity of human nature and relationships. By distinguishing shared qualities and unique idiosyncrasies, we acquire a greater understanding of the complex and ever-evolving nature of human behavior.

# Chapter 7

# Applying Behavioral Understanding

Understanding human behavior sets the basis for successful communication. In this chapter, we investigate personalized communication tactics that resonate with varied behavioral types, strengthening interpersonal relationships and decreasing misunderstandings.

## *Communication Strategies:*

*1. Adaptability:* Tailor communication approaches to reflect the preferences of varied behavioral types, ensuring that messages connect well with people across the spectrum.

**_2. Active Listening_**: Cultivate the talent of active listening to comprehend the intricacies of others' speech, building a culture of mutual understanding and respect.

**_3. Clarity and Transparency:_** Emphasize clear and transparent communication to reduce ambiguity, ensuring that information is delivered in a manner that satisfies both analytical and expressive preferences.

**_4. Empathy:_** Infuse empathy into communication by examining the emotional context of communications, and acknowledging the value of connecting on a human level.

**_5. Flexibility in Expression:_** Encourage a range of communication modalities, allowing for written, spoken, and visual expressions to meet varied communication preferences.

**_6. Conflict Resolution abilities_**: Equip people with the ability to handle disputes by recognizing the underlying behavioral dynamics and supporting constructive discussion.

# *Team Dynamics*

Navigating team dynamics involves a grasp of the unique capabilities and contributions that people with different behavior types bring to the table. This section covers ways to develop cohesive and productive teams.

*1. Variety Appreciation*: Foster an atmosphere that recognizes and respects the variety of behavioral types within the team, acknowledging the unique talents each member provides.

*2. Collaborative Platforms*: Utilize collaborative platforms and activities that cater to varied behavioral inclinations, establishing a collective and inclusive team culture.

3*. __Role Flexibility:__* Embrace flexibility in allocating roles and tasks, realizing that people may thrive in various elements of a project depending on their behavioral strengths.

*4. __Communication standards:__* Establish clear communication standards within the team, ensuring that all members feel comfortable sharing their thoughts and concerns.

*5. __Feedback methods:__* Implement feedback methods that adapt to varied communication types, encouraging a culture of continual improvement and open communication.

*6. __Recognition and Appreciation__*: Recognize and appreciate the efforts of team members, appreciating the unique ways in which different behavioral types contribute to team success.

# <u>*Leadership Approaches*</u>

Effective leadership entails changing one's leadership style to the demands and preferences of the team members. This section covers leadership tactics that connect with distinct behavior patterns.

**<u>1. Adaptable Leadership:</u>** Adopt an adaptable leadership style that flexibly reacts to the requirements and preferences of individual team members, acknowledging the range of behavioral attributes.

**<u>2. Inclusive Decision-Making:</u>** Encourage inclusive decision-making procedures that include input from persons with varied behavioral inclinations, generating a feeling of ownership and commitment.

**<u>3. Clear Vision Communication:</u>** Clearly explain the vision and objectives of the team or company, matching communications with the values and ambitions that resonate with varied behavioral types.

**_4. Mentorship and Development:_** Provide mentorship and development opportunities suited to individual strengths and growth areas, understanding that various behavioral types may benefit from varying methods of leadership development.

**_5. Conflict Resolution Skills:_** Develop and model effective conflict resolution skills, providing an example for the team on how to handle differences with respect and understanding.

**_6. Criticism and acknowledgment:_** Offer constructive criticism and acknowledgment in a way that matches the preferences of various behavioral types, ensuring that leadership communication is powerful and motivating.

This chapter tries to bridge the gap between knowing human behavior and implementing that knowledge successfully in communication, team dynamics, and leadership, promoting cultures that celebrate variety and maximize the collective potential of people.

# Chapter 8

# Challenges and Opportunities in Behavioral Diversity

As we examine the diverse terrain of behavioral variety, this chapter looks into the inherent obstacles and bountiful possibilities that occur in the rich fabric of human relationships. Navigating the intricacies of varied behaviors demands a comprehensive awareness of both the difficulties that may develop and the possibilities for collective achievement via embracing variety.

## *Navigating Conflicts:*

Conflicts are an unavoidable element of human relationships, and knowing how varied behaviors contribute to conflicts is crucial for resolution. This section digs into the complexity of handling disputes within the framework of behavioral variety.

**_1. Behavioral Awareness_**: Encourage folks to reflect on their behavioral patterns and notice them in others. Increased awareness allows a better knowledge of the possible origins of conflict.

**_2. Active Listening:_** Emphasize the significance of active listening as a core skill for conflict resolution. Understanding other views is crucial to establishing common ground and resolving disagreements.

**_3. Adaptable Communication_**: Explore the notion of altering communication techniques during disagreements. Tailoring communication to the preferences of others aids in de-escalation and creates a more fruitful discourse.

**_4. Mediation Strategies:_** Introduce mediation approaches that build on the strengths of distinct behavioral types. A mediator with an awareness of varied behaviors may handle disputes more successfully.

**_5. Conflict Resolution Models:_** Present proven conflict resolution models that address the complexity of human behavior. Models like the Win-Win strategy may be developed to secure a mutually beneficial outcome.

**_6. Building a Conflict-Resilient Culture:_** Propose techniques for companies to develop a culture that perceives disagreements as opportunities for progress. Encouraging open communication and learning from disagreements adds to a resilient and adaptable workplace.

# *Leveraging Diversity for Success:*

While problems exist, variation in behavior also gives a multitude of opportunities for accomplishment. This section addresses how accepting and using varied behaviors may push people and organizations toward higher success.

***1. Innovation and Creativity:*** Highlight the value of varied viewpoints in encouraging innovation and creativity. A blend of behavioral features may lead to more thorough problem-solving and inventive solutions.

***2. Adaptive Problem-Solving:*** Illustrate how varied actions contribute to adaptive problem-solving. Each behavior type delivers a distinct approach, boosting the overall flexibility of people and teams.

***3. Enhanced Decision-Making***: Discuss the advantages of varied decision-making methods. By examining a diversity of viewpoints, decision-making becomes more robust and reflective of various ideas.

***4. Dynamic Team Performance:*** Explore how teams made of people with varying behaviors may adjust dynamically to changing obstacles, contributing to total team performance.

5***. Cultural competency:*** Emphasize the relevance of cultural competency in harnessing behavioral diversity. Understanding and valuing varied behaviors lead to a more inclusive and culturally competent workplace.

***6. Employee Engagement:*** Showcase how accepting behavioral diversity adds to better levels of employee engagement. Recognizing and respecting individual contributions builds a good and inclusive workplace culture.

This chapter tries to help readers through the nuances of both obstacles and possibilities given by behavioral variety. By negotiating disputes with elegance and harnessing diversity for success, people and organizations may unleash the full potential of their dynamic human tapestry.

# Conclusion

# Summing Up Behavioral Diversity

In closing our investigation of behavioral variety, we find ourselves standing within a diverse tapestry of human experiences and relationships. The complicated patterns woven by analytical, pleasant, expressive, and driven actions show a fascinating tapestry that defies easy categorizations. As we ponder on the many expressions of human conduct, it becomes obvious that each behavioral type adds distinctive colors to the collective painting of mankind.

Our trip through the chapters has shown the dynamic interaction of nature and nurture, historical viewpoints, and the intricacies of individual and overlapping qualities. Understanding behavioral variety goes beyond basic awareness; it includes a thorough respect for the intricacies that affect how people see, behave, and contribute to the world around them. By accepting this variety, we unleash a pool of potential for establishing meaningful relationships, generating innovation, and collaboratively managing the complexity of our common life.

This investigation serves as an encouragement to consider behavioral variation not as a task to conquer but as a source of strength and richness. It urges us to approach every connection with inquiry and empathy, realizing that the variations inside us are the threads that weave the tapestry of our common human experience.

## ***Encouraging Inclusivity:***

## Human Nature Unveiled

As we end our voyage across the worlds of behavioral variety, the demand for supporting inclusion resounds with great relevance. Inclusivity is not only a nod to differences but a celebration of the numerous ways in which people display their distinct behavioral patterns. It is an assertion that the richness of our collective tapestry comes from the awareness and appreciation of varied ideas, methods, and identities.

Encouraging inclusion goes beyond simple awareness of diversity; it includes deliberately establishing circumstances where each behavioral type is not only recognized but also celebrated for the variety it contributes. In an inclusive setting, people feel seen, heard, and respected, establishing a feeling of belonging that transcends behavioral categorizations.

Our path through understanding behavioral variety culminates in the notion that real inclusion is a fuel for cooperation, creativity, and communal progress. It is a dedication to developing situations where every person, regardless of their behavioral proclivities, has the chance to grow, contribute, and be a vital part of the ever-evolving human tapestry.